Giggle Fit™

Dinosaur Jokes

CHICAGO PUBLIC LIBRARY
ROGERS PARK BRANCH
6807-17 N. CLARK ST
CHICAGO, IL 60626

D1227031

Illustrated by
Steve Harpster

Jacqueline Horsfall

Sterling Publishing Co., Inc.
New York

JUVE
PN6231
.D65
H67
2003

Library of Congress Cataloging-in-Publication Data Available

10 9 8 7 6 5 4 3 2 1

Published in paperback 2004 by Sterling Publishing Co., Inc.
387 Park Avenue South, New York, N.Y. 10016
© 2003 by Jacqueline Horsfall
Distributed in Canada by Sterling Publishing
^{c}/o Canadian Manda Group, One Atlantic Avenue, Suite 105
Toronto, Ontario, Canada M6K 3E7
Distributed in Great Britain by Chris Lloyd at Orca
Book Services, Stanley House, Fleets Lane, Poole BH15 3AJ, England
Distributed in Australia by Capricorn Link (Australia) Pty. Ltd.
P.O. Box 704, Windsor, NSW 2756 Australia
Printed in China
All rights reserved

Sterling ISBN 1-4027-0441-0 Hardcover
ISBN 1-4027-1761-X Paperback

R03022 32068

ROGERS PARK BRANCH
69   ARK ST
C   AGO, IL 60626

DISCARD

How do you talk to a dinosaur?
Use big words.

Knock-Knock.
Who's there?
Dozen.
Dozen who?
**Dozen anyone want to
see my pet dinosaur?**

What's as big as a dinosaur
but weighs nothing?
A dinosaur's shadow.

Why did the dinosaur sit on the bus?
It was too big to sit IN the bus.

What would you have if a dinosaur sat on your room?
A mush-room.

What did Humpty Dumpty do when a dinosaur sat on him?
Called 911 on his shell phone.

What does a Triceratops sit on?
Its Tricera-bottom.

What vegetable do you get if a dinosaur
sits on your dinner plate?
Squash.

How would you feel if a dinosaur fell on you?
Very, very dino-sore.

Why don't dinosaurs have wings?
They like chicken nuggets better.

What do dinosaurs eat with their cheeseburgers?
Dragonfries.

What do you get if a dinosaur sits on your French fries?
Mashed potatoes.

What do dinosaurs eat on cruises?
Fish and ships.

On which day does a Tyrannosaurus eat people?
Chewsday.

Why does a Tyrannosaurus eat raw meat?
It never learned how to cook.

Why do dinosaurs eat snowmen?
They melt in the mouth.

What happens when a dinosaur sneezes?
It blows your mind.

What direction does a dinosaur sneeze travel?
Atchoo!

What should you do when a dinosaur sneezes?
Get out of the way.

Why don't many dinosaurs celebrate their birthdays? **Two-hundred million candles won't fit on the cake.**

Why don't dinosaurs ski? **No one sells size 3000 ski boots.**

Why don't dinosaurs take ballet lessons? **They're just tutu big.**

Where was the dinosaur
when the sun went down?
In the dark.

What does a dinosaur
get if it drops jam on its
tummy?
A jellybutton.

What do you do if you find a
sleepy dinosaur in your
peanut butter sandwich?
Read it a breadtime story.

What do you call a
sleeping dinosaur?
A Stegosnorus.

What do dinosaurs
sleep on?
Bedrock.

How do you know there's a dinosaur
at your sleepover?
It has a D on its pajamas.

What do dinosaurs have that no other animals have?
Baby dinosaurs.

How would you find dinosaur eggs?
Go on an eggspedition.

What do baby dinosaurs use to get out of their eggs?
Hatch-ets.

What did the Stegosaurus use to build its dog house?
A dino-saw.

What's the best way to raise a dinosaur?
With a crane.

How fast did the dinosaur get back to its nest of eggs?
It scrambled.

What should you do if you find a dinosaur in your bathtub?

Pull out the plug!

How do dinosaurs bathe?

They take meteor showers.

How can you tell if there's a dinosaur in your shower?

You can't close the curtain.

Why do dinosaurs shower with mice?
So they'll be squeaky clean.

Why do dinosaurs take
showers?
To get ex-stinked.

What time does a
Tyrannosaurus get up?
Ate o'clock.

What would happen if a dinosaur sat in front of you at the theater?
You'd miss the whole movie!

How can you tell if a Tyrannosaurus has been to the movies?
By the popcorn stuck in its teeth.

What should you do if a dinosaur burps pepperoni breath in your face?
Give it a pizza your mind.

Why did the Tyrannosaurus go to school?

It heard the cafeteria was serving Baked Beings.

What does a Tyrannosaurus like eating most in the school cafeteria?

The lunch tables.

What's a dinosaur's favorite class?

Mashematics.

How did the little dinosaurs like their first day at preschool?

They had a bawl.

What time is it when ten dinosaurs chase you in your sleep?
Ten after one.

How did the Velociraptor move so fast?
It ran through quicksand.

Why can't we hide from a Tyrannosaurus?
Because the dino saw us.

What's the fastest way to get to the hospital?
Pick a fight with a Velociraptor.

Why did the Apatosaurus cross the road?
Because the Tyrannosaurus ate the chicken.

What happens when dinosaurs run out of firecrackers?
They use dino-mite.

How can you tell if a
dinosaur is a vegetarian?
Lie down on a plate.

Why does a Tyrannosaurus
chase its prey?
It loves fast food.

What does a Tyrannosaurus call a car full of people?
A lunch box.

What does a Brachiosaurus
eat every morning?
Brachfast.

Why can't dinosaurs keep secrets?
They have big mouths.

How do you ask a Tyrannosaurus to lunch?
"Tea, Rex?"

What treat do dinosaurs
make over a campfire?
Dino-s'mores.

What happened when the
Tyrannosaurus met the Apatosaurus?
It was love at first bite.

What game should you never play
with a dinosaur?
Leap frog.

Why couldn't the
dinosaur play games
on the computer?
**The Tyrannosaurus
ate the mouse.**

What's a dinosaur's favorite dance?
The Stomp.

Where did the Tyrannosaurus go to dance?
To the Meat Ball.

How did the King's men find Cinderellasaurus after the ball?
They followed her Foot Prince.

How do we know dinosaurs flossed their teeth?

Scientists found the flossils.

What does a Tyrannosaurus swear in court?

To tell "the tooth, the whole tooth, and nothing but the tooth."

What's so great about dinosaur teeth?

They're totally gnawsome.

What time is it when a Tyrannosaurus
visits the dentist?
Tooth-hurty.

What happens when Tyrannosauruses
visit the dentist?
They're nervous rex.

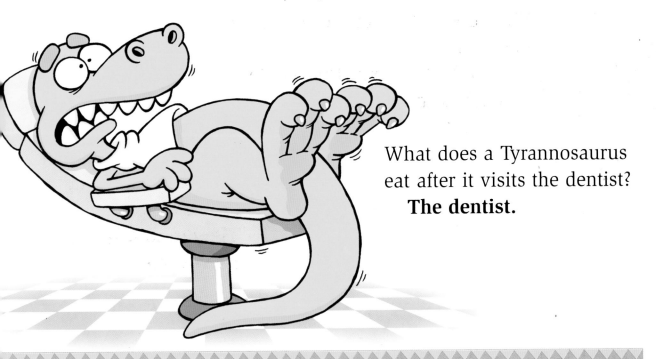

What does a Tyrannosaurus
eat after it visits the dentist?
The dentist.

What does a Tyrannosaurus do when it exercises?
Crunches.

Where can you find dinosaurs at the playground?
On the rock-slide.

How much do dinosaur bones weigh?
Skele-tons.

What size T-shirt do dinosaurs wear?

XXXXXXXXXXXXXX-Large.

What does an Apatosaurus wear to aerobics class?

Sweatplants.

Where does a Tyrannosaurus keep its sneakers?

In the bedroom claws-it.

What was the
Apatosaurus doing
on the highway?
**About two
miles per hour.**

Where does an Apatosaurus
fill up?
At the grass-station.

What does a Tyrannosaurus
say when introduced?
"Pleased to eat you."

What do you use to see distant dinosaurs?
Dinoculars.

Where do cows go to see dinosaur skeletons?
To moo-seums.

Which vegetable is helpful in finding dinosaur bones?
Clue-cumbers.

What do you call dinosaur skeletons lying on the ground?
Lazy bones.

What kind of dinosaurs live at the North Pole?
Cold ones!

What do you call a dinosaur at the South Pole?
Lost.

What's a T. Rex at the North Pole called?
Iced T.

Why doesn't Stegosaurus
play when it rains?
Because Stegosau-rust.

Who brings
Tyrannosaurus
presents on
Christmas Eve?
Santa Claws.

What do dinosaurs wear under
their raincoats?
Thunderwear.

Why can't dinosaurs go swimming?
The elephants have all the trunks.

What happens when a dinosaur
goes swimming?
It gets wet.

Do dinosaurs like going to
the beach?
They shore do.

What should you wear to Dinosaur Beach?
Sunscream.

Where do reptiles apply their sunscreen?
On their rep-tails.

What do you call a dinosaur on your pool chair?
The Big Dripper.

How would you feel if you
saw real live dinosaurs?
Very, very old.

On which side does a Stegosaurus
have the most scales?
The outside.

Why don't dinosaurs have antennae?
Because they get cable.

How big is a
dinosaur picnic?
Enormess.

How can you tell if a Stegosaurus is going
on a picnic?
By the plates on its back.

What happens when dinosaurs picnic
on top of volcanoes?
They have a blast.

Why don't dinosaurs drive convertibles?
Their heads bump the traffic lights.

How do you get a
Triceratops' attention?
Honk its horn.

What do you call a dinosaur
that never gives up?
Try-try-try-ceratops.

What happened when dinosaurs
started driving?
**They had Tyrannosaurus
Wrecks.**

Where do dinosaurs
park their jeeps?
**In Jurassic
Parking lots.**

How do dinosaurs fly
from coast to coast?
On jumbo jets.

How can you tell if there's a dinosaur under your bed?
Your nose bumps the ceiling.

What does a dinosaur use to clean the kitchen floor?
Tricera-mops.

In what age did dinosaurs refuse to clean their rooms?
The Messy-zoic period.

What would you do if you found a dinosaur in your bed?
Sleep on the sofa.

Did you hear about the turkey dinosaur?
It gobbles you up.

What does a Tyrannosaurus eat at Sunday dinner?
Roast beast.

What do dinosaurs like to do at parties?
Crash them.

Why do dinosaurs have
wrinkled skin?
**They don't have
time to iron.**

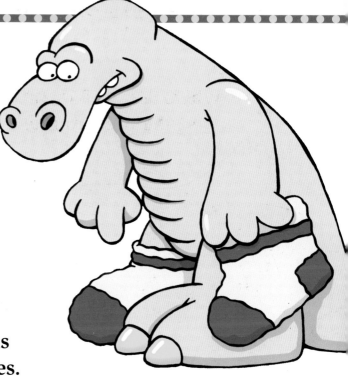

How do dinosaurs
count to 2?
**Take off their socks
and count their toes.**

Why did the dinosaur paint her toenails red?
So she could hide in the strawberry patch.

Why do dinosaurs' earrings keep falling off?
They don't have any earlobes.

Where does a Tyrannosaurus find its meat?
At the preyground.

What do dinosaurs
eat on their cactus
sandwiches?
Dill prickles.

How do dinosaurs like
their chicken?
Petrifried.

Which dinosaur knocks at your door?
The rap-rap-raptor!

What good is a dinosaur's snout?

It nose how to find you.

What do you have if a Tyrannosaurus gets mad at your cat?

A real cat-astrophe.

What's the difference between a dinosaur and a flea?
About 50 tons.

How do dinosaurs fight?
With dino-swords.

Which dinosaur wears a ten-gallon hat?
Tyrannosaurus Tex.

What kind of horse does Tyrannosaurus Tex ride?
A bronco-saurus.

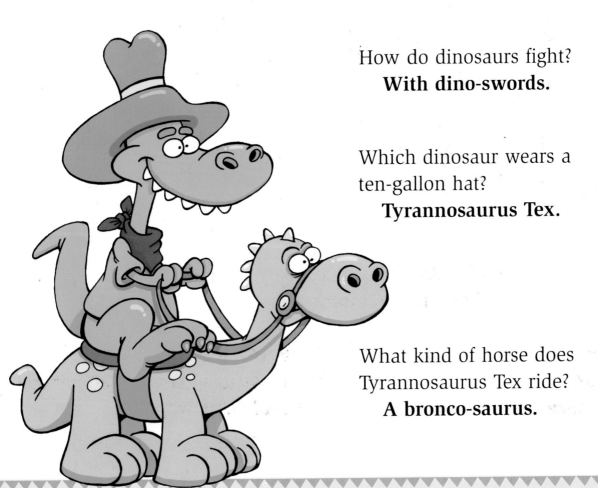

What is Dracula's favorite dinosaur?
The Terror-dactyl.

Who is Harry Pottersaurus?
The Lizard Wizard.

What's an Elvisaurus?
**The King of the
Dinosaurs.**

What would you get if you crossed a dinosaur with a lemon?

A dinosour.

What would you get if you crossed a dinosaur with a skunk?

A Stinkosaurus.

Which dinosaurs sing and dance on MTV?

Rap-tors.

Knock-Knock.
　Who's there?
Gopher.
　Gopher who?
Gopher help! There's a
dinosaur in my bed!

Knock-Knock.
　Who's there?
Dinosaur go.
　Dinosaur go who?
No, owls go whoo . . .
dinosaurs go RRRAAAAHHH!

Knock-Knock.
　Who's there?
Canoe.
　Canoe who?
Canoe help me get this
dinosaur out of my canoe?

46

How do you know dinosaurs traveled in groups?
I herd it.

Why is a dinosaur's
tail always dirty?
It's a real drag.

How does a Tyrannosaurus
say goodbye?
"Catch you later!"

INDEX